Practical
Karate

Defense Against Multiple Assailants

Practical
Karate 3

Defense Against Multiple Assailants

M. Nakayama
Donn F. Draeger

Tuttle Publishing
Boston • Rutland, Vermont • Tokyo

Disclaimer
The adoption and application of the material offered in this book is at the reader's discretion and sole responsibility. The Author and Publisher of this book are not responsible in any manner whatsoever for any injury that may occur indirectly or directly from the use of this book. Since the physical activities described herein may be too strenuous in nature for some readers to engage in safely, please consult a physician prior to training. The specific self-defense practices illustrated in this book may not be justified in every particular situation or under applicable federal, state or local law. Neither the Author or the Publisher make any warranty or representation regarding the legality or appropriateness of any technique mentioned in this book.

Library of Congress Catalog Card Number: 98-87646
ISBN 0-8048-0483-4

DISTRIBUTED BY

NORTH AMERICA
Tuttle Publishing
RR 1 Box 231-5
North Clarendon, VT 05759
Tel: (802) 773-8930
Tel: (800) 526-2778

SOUTHEAST ASIA
Berkeley Books Pte. Ltd.
5 Little Road #08-01
Singapore 536983
Tel: (65) 280-3320
Fax: (65) 280-6290

JAPAN
Tuttle Shokai Ltd.
1-21-13, Seki
Tama-ku, Kawasaki-shi
Kanagawa-ken 214, Japan
Tel: (044) 833-0225
Fax: (044) 822-0413

First edition
07 06 05 04 03 02 01   00 99 98   10 9 8 7 6 5 4 3 2 1

Printed in Singapore

TABLE OF CONTENTS

Authors' Foreword 7

Preface 9

Essential Points 12

Chapter One: ATTACKS AGAINST STANDING POSITIONS
. . . . 13

> *Frontal Wrist Seizures (level ground); Frontal Wrist Seizures (elevated position); Rear Collar and Wrist Seizures; Full Nelson and Search; Rear Bear Hug and Frontal Striking; Rear Hammerlock and Striking; Rear Tackle and Striking; Scaling and Striking; Front and Rear Free Threat; Frontal Free Threat; Frontal Lapel Seizure and Striking; Frontal Free Threat, Striking, and Kicking; Rear Collar Seizure and Frontal Striking; Side Holding and Frontal Kicking.*

Chapter Two: ATTACKS AGAINST SITTING POSITIONS . 83

> *Seated Frontal Lapel Seizure and Striking; Seated Frontal Free Threat and Striking; Rear Chair Holding and Frontal Threat; Pull Out of Chair and Frontal Striking.*

Chapter Three: ATTACKS AGAINST LYING POSITIONS . 103

> *Frontal Lapel Seizure and Foot Trip; Frontal Push Down Against Wall and Attack; Ground Choking and Kicking Attack.*

AUTHORS' FOREWORD

THERE IS, perhaps, no greater disservice to man than the creation of false confidence in his ability to defend himself. Whether this false confidence is manifested in his nations' armed might, or in his own personal ability, the result is the same, though of different proportions, when tested . . . DISASTER!

The current *karate* "boom" in the U.S.A. has instilled in many would-be "experts" a serious, false sense of security. This is the natural outgrowth of a human psychological weakness. Everyone wishes to be physically fit and able to defend himself and his loved ones from danger, and quickly turns to any sure-fire guarantee of such abilities.

Unscrupulous and unqualified self-appointed *karate* "experts" daily exploit this human weakness and prey on an innocent, unsuspecting public. This grossly perpetrated fraud is based on the quick learning of ancient mysterious Oriental combative forms such as *karate,* and almost always makes its appeal through colorful adjectives such as "super," destructive," "terror tactics," and guarantees you mastery which will make you "fear no man." All such "get skillful quickly" schemes should be carefully investigated before choosing, for true *karate* involves constant dedication to training and is never a "short course" method. Choose your instructor carefully.

On the other hand, authentic teachers of *karate* do exist in the U.S.A., and their teachings have full merit. These teachings are deeply rooted in tradition, classical *karate* and require a liberal application of patience and regular training to develop expert *karate* skill. There are various schools which stem from historic Oriental antiquity, all of which are legitimate and have both merits and shortcomings. The choice of which school to follow can be decided upon only by the interested party.

The average person is confined to a daily life which requires of him a heavy investment in time and energy in order to earn a living. Leisure time is generally at a minimum and spent at less enervating pursuits than demanded by classical *karate* practice. But the need for a practical system of self-defense designed for the average person is more evident than ever before. Police files give mute testimony to the increasing number of robberies, assaults, and other vicious crimes.

Like its predecessor, Volume Two, this book is a categorized collection of self-defense situations and recommended *karate* responses. It is written for every male and brings to him a chance to improve his personal self-defense abilities without engaging in the daily training required by classical *karate*. It is not an exhaustive survey of *karate* methods, but chooses methods which are easy to learn. All methods described in this book are workable *karate* self-defense responses based on meeting multiple unarmed assailants.

If you have already studied and practiced the necessary *karate* fundamentals found in Volume One of this series, the situations in this volume will be easy to learn. Otherwise, after reading about the situation and response herein, you may find it necessary to turn to Volume One and study the required movements.

The reader is reminded that even mastery of the techniques in this text *will not* make him invincible in personal encounters, but it will certainly better prepare him for common eventualities should defense of his life or that of others become necessary.

The authors are indebted to the Japan Karate Association, Tokyo, for the use of their facilities and acknowledge with pleasure the assistance of their members who have made this book possible. Additional thanks is due Kazuo Obata and his excellent photographic skills, and to Kenneth L. Busch, William A. Fuller, C. Nicol, George Hoff, and Charles Marah, who have posed as the "assailants."

PREFACE

KARATE is a martial art developed by people who were prohibited the use of weapons, thus making it a *defensive* art. When one is attacked, the empty hands (which the word *karate* implies) are quite sufficient to defend oneself if one is highly skilled in the art. However, to become highly skilled takes exacting discipline, both mental and physical. The main purpose of this series of four books is to avoid the advanced techniques of *karate* which require many years of study and instead to describe simplified *karate* technique as easy-to-learn responses to typical self-defense situations.

Karate is highly esteemed as a sport, self-defense, and as a physical attribute for athletics in general. It is becoming increasingly popular in schools, offices, factories, law enforcement agencies and the armed services, varying in degree as required by the respective wants and needs.

In response to the many requests for treatment of *karate* purely as a defensive system, it is hoped that the information contained in this series of four books will be more than sufficient to meet these requests. In conclusion, if readers of this series of books will fully understand the principles and ideals of *karate*, taking care to use its techniques with discretion, they will reflect great credit to this magnificent art.

ZENTARO KOSAKA
Former Foreign Minister
of Japan
Director, Japan Karate Association

9

THE FIRST and most complete and authoritative text on *karate* in the English language, titled *Karate: The Art of "Empty Hand" Fighting,* by Hidetake Nishiyama and Richard C. Brown, instructor and member of the Japan Karate Association respectively, made its appearance in 1960. It presents *karate* in its three main aspects—a healthful physical art, an exciting sport, and an effective form of self-defense. As such, it is considered the standard textbook of the Japan Karate Association and adequately serves both as a reference and instructional manual for novice and expert alike.

Many students of *karate* find the study of classical *karate* somewhat impractical in modern Western society, chiefly because time limitations prohibit sufficient practice. These students generally desire to limit their interpretations of *karate* to self-defense aspects. With this sole training objective in mind, a series of four volumes is being prepared which describes in simplified form, the necessary *karate* movements for personal defense that can be learned by anybody of average physical abilities.

The authors, M. Nakayama, Chief Instructor of the Japan Karate Association and Donn F. Draeger, a well-known instructor of combative arts, bring a balanced, practical, and functional approach to *karate,* based on the needs of Western society. As a specialized series of *karate* texts, these are authentic books giving full and minute explanations of the practical art of self-defense. All movements are performed in normal daily dress and bring the performer closer to reality.

Today, *karate* is attracting the attention of the whole world and is being popularized at an amazing rate. I sincerely hope that this series of books will be widely read as a useful reference for the lovers of *karate* all over the world. It is further hoped that the techniques shown in this series of books need never be used by any reader, but should an emergency arise making their use unavoidable, discretion in application should be the keynote.

MASATOMO TAKAGI
Standing Director and
Head of the General Affairs
Department of the Japan
Karate Association

Practical
Karate

*Defense Against
Multiple Assailants*

ESSENTIAL POINTS

1. Never underestimate your assailants. Always assume that they are dangerous.

2. Stepping, weight shifting, and body turning are the keys to avoiding the assailants' attack and bringing them into position for your counterattack.

3. Turn your body as a unit, not in isolated parts, for maximum effect.

4. If the ground is rough, bumpy, or slick, you may be unable to maneuver as you would like. Simple weight shifting and twisting of your hips may be all that is possible. Don't get too fancy in your footwork.

5. Your body can only act efficiently in *karate* techniques if you make it a stable foundation, working from braced feet and a balanced position as you deliver your blows.

6. Coordinate your blocking or striking actions to the assailants' target areas with your stepping, weight shifting, and body turning for maximum effect.

7. Do not oppose superior power with power, but seek to harmonize it with your body action and direct it to your advantage.

8. Seek to deliver your striking actions to each assailant's anatomical weak points (vital points) rather than to hard, resistant areas.

9. After delivering the striking action to one assailant's target area, you must not lose sight of him as you deal with the other assailant. You must constantly be on the alert for a continuation of attack by either or both parties.

10. Use discretion in dealing out punishment to the assailants. Fit the degree of punishment to the situation.

Chapter One
ATTACKS AGAINST
STANDING POSITIONS

UNARMED ASSAILANTS working in pairs or small groups commonly attack with methods that include seizing, holding the arms, portions of the garments, hugging, choking, and tackling by one or two persons, while the second or other members of the small group endeavor to threaten you with further violence that includes searching, punching or striking, kneeing or kicking, or combinations of these methods. All can be used with effective results against an untrained person.

Self-defense situations which involve you with two or more unarmed assailants using these tactics are obviously delicate situations in which an improper response by you may result in serious injury or loss of life.

The person highly trained in *karate* techniques is able to meet such emergencies with confidence, yet there is a considerable difference between the highly trained and the average citizen. The situations and the appropriate responses shown in this chapter have been especially selected for the average person and cover the necessary principles to successfully meet common eventualities resulting from attacks by multiple unarmed assailants in a standing position.

As in Volume Two, the responses described must be practiced with partners. Regulate the initial practices carefully, by peforming the necessary moveents in slow motion until you understand the exact peformance completely. Gradually increase the speed of the situation and the appropriate response as your training partners "attack" you. Seek to build automatic responses. Frequent practice (a few minutes) a day several days a week), will aid this development.

All practice should be made in normal daily dress. Do not make the mistake of practicing only on a smooth, flat surface such as a gym floor, but try to make these responses on grass, gravel, and paved and unpaved surfaces so that you will be prepared for the situation as it could really happen.

While the responses in this chapter are given in terms of one side (either the right or left sides), in most instances the other side may be learned by simply reversing the instructions.

A final word about the execution of the responses to multiple assailant attacks. Deal directly with the assailant who poses the biggest threat *first*. In free threat situations, those situations in which no contact has been made, it is the *closest* assailant. Get rid of him first! In situations where you are being restrained by one or two assailants while the other or others are preparing to attack, it may also be the closest assailant who poses the biggest threat, but often it is not. Assailants who merely hold you can often, momentarily, be thought of as "out of action," as their full attention is concentrated on just holding you. In these cases, deal first with the other or others who are free and closing in on you Regardless of your plan of action, *never* assume that your first response will satisfy the situation. Rather assume a constant alertness which will enable you to continue your attack should it become necessary. The price of a lack of alertness may be your life! Generally the responses of this book are directed only to one target area, but other opportunities should be studied.

Situation: You have been gripped by two assailants, each of whom has double-gripped one of your wrists. They try to twist your wrists and force you into submission.

Response: Shift your weight quickly onto your left foot, bending your left knee slightly. Raise your right foot off of the ground and bend your right knee so that your thigh is parallel to the ground. Keep some tension in your arms to assist you in maintaining your balance. (See left picture above.) Drive your right Foot Edge, hard, diagonally downward into your right hand assailant's nearest leg, anywhere from the knee down to the instep. (See pictures, this page.)

Immediately after this kicking action, return your right foot to the ground, bend that knee slightly, and shift your weight quickly to it. Then raise your left foot off the ground, bending your left knee so that your thigh is parallel to the ground. (See pictures above.) Drive your left Foot Edge, hard, diagonally downward into your left hand assailant's nearest leg anywhere from the knee down to the instep. The final action can be seen on page 18.

Key Points: Your balance during kicking actions will be easy to maintain if your assailants hold on to your wrists. By tugging or releasing yourself, you destroy your best chance to attack, and increase their offensive capabilities. Your first kicking action may cause one assailant to release his wrist hold on you, and you must be alert for any continuation of his attack with other tactics. If you combine this double-kicking action into smooth movements, it is possible to deliver a series of quick kicks, alternating sides, to render harmless the most difficult and insistent assailants. Do not sway from side to side during kicking actions.

Situation: You have been seized by two assailants, each of whom has double-gripped one of your wrists (arms). They attack you on a stairway, one assailant below you, the other above, attempting to bring you into submission.

Response: Place your left foot high side securely on a tread of the stairway and quickly shift your weight to that foot, bending your left knee slightly. Lift your right leg high and thread it over the lower assailant's left arm from the outside. (See pictures above.) Drive your right Foot Edge hard between the lower assailant's arms, straight into his midsection. (Follow picture sequence.)

As you complete your kicking action on the lower assailant, speedily bring your right leg close to your body, knee bent, thigh parallel to the ground. You will have to twist your hips a bit to the left and pivot on your left foot to do this. (See pictures above.) Drive the ball of your right foot hard into the groin region of the upper assailant, or to any vital area (knee, shin) lower down. The final action can be seen on page 22.

Key Points: You must attack the lower assailant first as his chance of unbalancing you is the greatest. Prior to delivering your kick against him, get as high as you can (near to the high-side assailant) so that you can thread your right leg more easily. Your kicking action should aim at the assailant's midsection, but may center hard against his arms, thus breaking his grip. After this first kick, you must very quickly deliver your second kick. Do not allow yourself to be balanced on one leg, thus giving the upper assailant a chance to upset you.

22

Situation: You have been seized by two assailants, each of whom has taken your wrist with one hand from the rear, and the back of your collar with his other hand. They are walking you against your will.

Response: Do not tug to release yourself, but rather seek to blend with their movements which are forcing you forward. Select either assailant to attack first (right shown) and get into step with him. Weight your left leg as you step forward with that foot, raising your right leg, knee bent, so that your right thigh is parallel to the ground. (See pictures above.)

24

Keep some tension in your arms to assist you in keeping your balance, and drive a hard right Foot Edge backward into the knee of the assailant on your right rear side. (See top picture.) This action can be seen fully in the large picture above.

At this kick, your assailant will release his grip on you. Immediately step your kicking right foot to a position at your right rear as shown in the diagram. As you do this, raise your now free right arm across your body and position your right hand, palm down, at your left shoulder. (See large picture above.)

With a snap-twist of your hips to your right, chop your right elbow hard into the other assailant's ribs or midsection. (Follow pictures across the top of these two pages.) This action can be seen from a different angle in the picture sequence above. The final action can be seen on page 28.

Key Points: Your first kicking attack must be to the assailant's nearest leg. To do this easily, you must get in step with him. Pulling him a bit forward as you kick will increase the effect. Your pivot and twist of your hips to the right as you deliver your right Elbow Sideward Strike will be increased if you lower your hips slightly by bending your knees. Note also that after your first kick your right knee is raised parallel to the ground once again prior to stepping for the pivot. During the pivotal action, pull your trapped left arm hard around with your hip action, keeping it close to your body.

Situation: One assailant has taken you into a Full Nelson and is holding you while another assailant searches your person for valuables.

29

Response: Do not struggle against the Full Nelson, but maintain your balance and brace your feet. Keep as upright as possible as the assailant to your front begins his searching. When he is occupied with his search, twist your hips quickly to your right, keeping your feet more-or-less in place, and drive a left Elbow Forward Strike into the temple or face area of your frontal assailant. (See pictures this page.)

Immediately shift your weight onto your left foot, bending that knee slightly, as you raise your right foot from the ground so that your thigh is parallel to the ground. Without hesitation drive your right heel or Foot Edge into the rear assailant's right shin and instep, with a hard snap. (See pictures above.) Pivot on your weighted left foot and step your right foot into position (see diagram) as the rear assailant releases his Full Nelson (after your kicking attack). Simultaneously, swing your right elbow around with the twist of your hips to the right and drive a hard Elbow Sideward Strike into the jaw of the rear assailant, keeping your right hand in a tight fist, palm down, as you deliver it. Your left hand is brought into a tight fist, palm up, at your left hip. This final action can be seen on page 32.

Key Points: You must attack the assailant to your front first and with enough accuracy and severity to drop him or keep him inactive as you work on the rear assailant. You must make the assailant to your front get his head as close as possible during the searching actions. Any premature attack on your part will spoil your chances. After dealing with the rear assailant, you must be alert for a continuation of the attack by your frontal assailant.

32

Situation: An assailant has seized you in a "bear hug" from the rear and is encircling both of your arms in an attempt to hold you while another assailant attacks you with his fists from the front.

33

Response: Do not struggle to free yourself from the rear "bear hug," but maintain your balance and keep alert, concen-
trating on the actions of your frontal assailant. At the first sign of his striking
attack, shift your weight onto your right
leg, bending that knee slightly. Quickly
raise your left foot off the ground and bend
your left knee so that your thigh is parallel
to the ground. (See upper picture above.)
Beat the frontal assailant to the punch by
snapping the ball of your left foot hard into
his groin area. (See above and top picture,
page 35.)

Immediately after this kicking action, swing your left leg back and step your left foot deeply between the rear assailant's legs, twisting your hips and pivoting to your left as shown in the pictures above and diagram· As you do this, swing both of your arms hard upward to loosen the rear assailant's "bear hug."

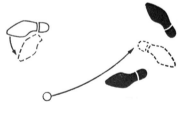

As your left foot comes between his legs, raise your right arm, hand held in a tight fist near your right ear. Fold your left arm across your body, hand held in a tight fist, palm down, in front of your chest. Simultaneously twist your body more to your left and drive your right fist, palm outward, into the face of the assailant as your left Elbow Sideward Strike smashes into his midsection. This final action can be seen on page 36.

Key Points: Your kicking attack at the frontal assailant must be timed as he comes into range, but before he can land his punch. If his groin region is difficult to reach, aim for his knee or shin. The swinging action of your left leg, after it finishes kicking the frontal assailant, is like a big pendulum which aids your body to turn to your left, thus breaking the rear assailant's "bear hug" and puts you into position for an attack against him. Blend it into one smooth movement. You may drive your left heel hard into your assailant's leg as you step between his legs, using it as a distraction to loosen him up for your final attack.

Situation: An assailant has seized your left arm in a hammerlock from the rear and is holding you while another assailant attacks you with his fists from the front.

37

Response: Do not struggle to free yourself from the hammerlock, but keep some tension in your captured arm to ease the pain. Keep your balance by lowering your hips and stepping back with your right foot and, as the frontal assailant throws a "haymaker" right at you, deflect it by performing a high right Rising Block against the outside of his right arm. (See picture to the left.) After you have deflected his blow and grasped his arm near his wrist, snap his arm downward with a grasping motion, pulling him forward, off balance, and into your right foot, snapping the ball of that foot hard into his midsection or groin region. (See below.)

After your kicking action against the frontal assailant, release your tight grasp and swing your right leg to your rear, pivoting and twisting as shown in the diagram. As you do this, fold your right arm across your body so that your hand is near your left ear, formed as a Knife-hand, palm inward. (Follow pictures above.) From a stable base formed by bracing your legs and lowering your hips a bit, chop a hard Knife-hand, using your right hand, into your rear assailant's rib area. This final action can be seen on page 40.

Key Points: The Rising Block will work against either arm the frontal assailant uses in his initial attack, but you must snap his arm downward as you kick. Your stepping and pivotal action as you attack the rear assailant must be done quickly, using the momentum of your entire body. Be alert for a continuation of the attack by both assailants, especially if your kick and Knife-hand attacks were badly timed or slightly off target. If your assailant is too close to use a Knife-hand, employ the Back or Bottom Fist, or in extremely close cases, your Elbow Sideward Strike.

Situation: You are aware of your frontal assailant who is menacing you with his fists. Suddenly you are tackled by a rear assailant and at the same time the frontal assailant punches at you.

Response: You are in a left Forward Stance preparing for the frontal assailant's attack when you are tackled from the rear. Keep your balance and drive a hard Rising Block, using your left arm against the inside of the frontal assailant's right punching action. Simultaneously bring your right arm alongside your right hip, hand held in a tight fist at your hip. (See left picture above.) Drop your hips a bit by bending your knees to facilitate keeping your balance and as the frontal assailant swings his left fist at you, perform a hard Forearm Block with your left arm against the inside of his striking left arm. Twist your hips to the right as you do this. (See right picture above.) With the same motion drive your right Bottom Fist to the rear assailant's ribs. (See upper picture, page 43.) With a snap of your left arm, slide your left Back Fist up the frontal assailant's left arm and strike him hard in the face or side of the head.

Pivot and twist your hips as shown in the diagram below, raising your right arm, elbow high, hand held in a tight fist vertically above your elbow, and smash your right Elbow Downward Strike into the rear assailant's kidney region or other suitable target (spine, base of head). The final action can be seen on page 44.

Key Points: Keeping your balance as you are tackled from the rear is of primary importance. If your frontal assailant is quite distant, or does not attack when the tackle is made, you may deal directly with the rear assailant first, but keep alert for the frontal attack. Using a kicking attack against the frontal assailant is dangerous in that it may seriously weaken your balance and make you easy to upset by the assailant tackling you. Your final elbow action can be in the form of an Elbow Sideward Strike if necessary. If the frontal assailant single punches (not shown) with his right hand, perform your Rising Block and Bottom Fist actions together as one motion.

44

Situation: An assailant has grabbed you from the rear, one hand on the back of your collar, the other reached between your legs and grabbing you by the crotch in an attempt to unbalance you and hold you. Another assailant is threatening to strike you from the front with his fists.

45

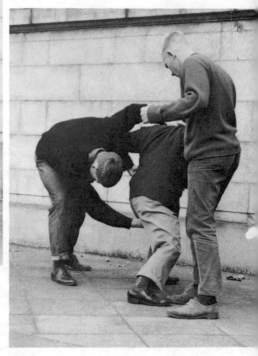

Response: At the first indication of the rear assailant's attack, keep your balance by lowering your hips. Bend your knees slightly to do this. Keep alert to the frontal assailant's attack and, before he can launch it, step quickly to the front with your right foot, toes pointing to your left. Bring your left arm across your body, hand held in a tight fist, palm inward. (See left picture above.) As your right foot comes into place, twist your body to the left and smash a hard left Elbow Sideward Strike into the rear assailant's ribs or midsection. (See right picture above.)

The pictures on this page show the action described on page 46 from a different angle.

The frontal assailant now closes in on you and swings a left fist at your head. Deflect this blow with your right arm by using a Downward Block against the inside of the frontal assailant's left arm. Your right arm comes from across your body, right fist near your right hip, palm inward. (See top picture above.) The picture above shows this action from another angle.

As the frontal assailant swings his right fist, deflect it with your right arm in the form of a Rising Block. (See top left picture.) The picture above shows this action from another angle. Shift your weight to your left leg, bending your left knee slightly as you raise your right leg, thigh parallel to the ground. (See top right picture.) Drive a hard right Foot Edge diagonally downward into the frontal assailant's right shin (knee or instep). The final action can be seen on page 50.

Key Points: Keeping your balance as you are being scaled from the rear is of primary importance. Using a kicking attack against the frontal assailant before you have dealt with the rear assailant is dangerous since this may seriously weaken your balance and make you easy to upset by the assailant scaling you. Be sure to lower your hips as you step forward to pivot into the rear assailant. After delivering your kick to the frontal assailant, be alert for a continuation of the rear assailant's attack.

50

Situation: You are aware of two assailants, one of whom is menacing you from the front with his fists, while the other is attacking you in a choking attempt from the rear.

Response: Take a right Forward Stance against the frontal assailant who is leading with his left fist. At the grasp of the rear assailant, quickly pivot your body to your left by pivoting your right foot a bit to the left and sliding your left foot around behind you. (See top picture and the diagram.) At the same time perform the Grasping Block against the frontal assailant's punching left arm from the outside, pulling him off balance to his right front. (Left picture.) Shift your weight to your right leg and raise your left leg off the ground, bending the knee so your thigh is parallel to the ground. (See right picture above.)

52

While keeping the frontal assailant off balance by pushing and pulling on his left arm, drive a hard left Foot Edge direct to the groin region of the rear assailant. (See top picture.) Without hesitation, quickly bring your kicking left foot alongside of your weighted right foot, shift your weight to the left leg, and free your right leg. Raise your right leg off the ground, bending the knee so your thigh is parallel to the ground as shown in the picture below and the diagram. Drive a hard right Foot Edge into the shin or instep of the frontal assailant's left leg. The final action can be seen on page 54.

Key Points: You must go into action before the rear assailant can seize you too firmly. Timing is essential here. After you have executed the Grasping Block against the frontal assailant, you must keep a push-pull effort on his captured left arm to keep him unbalanced and ineffective until you can deal with him. Holding his arm also aids your balance while you kick. If the rear assailant is too far away to be kicked as shown, cross step with your right foot in front of your left foot prior to kicking.

54

Situation: You are aware of two assailants. One is directly in view to your right front, while the other lurks in a semi-concealed position to your left front. The assailant to your right front tries to keep your attention.

Response: As you pass near him, the assailant on your left comes out of his semi-concealed position and swings at you with his right fist, or tries to grasp you with his right hand. Assume the Forward Stance by advancing your left leg, raising your left arm (bent at the elbow) over your right shoulder. Hold your left hand in a tight fist. (See left picture above.) Step forward a bit with your right foot as you swing your left arm against your assailant's right arm, using the Downward Block. Keep your right hand in a tight fist at your right hip. (See right picture above.)

56

As your assailant swings his left at you, step and pivot as shown in the diagram, and drive a Forearm Block with your right arm, hard against the punching left arm of your assailant. You must anticipate that the other assailant (formerly on your right) is now closing in from your rear. (See top large picture.) Shift your weight to your left leg, keeping a slightly bent knee, and deliver a hard Side Kick to the assailant's midsection as you grasp his left arm and pull him off balance. The other assailant is now within grasping range. (See above.)

57

Quickly step your kicking leg behind your weighted left leg, as shown in the upper left diagram, as you turn to meet the second assailant now getting ready to attack you from the rear. (See top left picture.) Shift your weight to your right leg, knee slightly bent, and raise your left leg, knee parallel to the ground. (See top right picture and diagram.) Drive your left leg hard into the second assailant, using the Side Kick, directly into his knee joint. (See picture above.)

As you finish your kicking action, step your left foot and pivot on your right foot as shown in the diagram above so that you face your second assailant in a Back Stance, left foot advanced. Keep your left arm in front of you to ward off his grasp as you raise your right arm, elbow bent, over your right shoulder, hand forming a Knife-hand. (See above left picture.) Twist your body forward, shifting to a Forward Stance as you swing your right Knife-hand hard into the face or neck area of your assailant. Simultaneously, bring your left hand, held in a tight fist, to your left hip, knuckles down. (See above right picture.) The final action may be seen on page 60.

Key Points: When an apparent single assailant tries hard to keep your attention, anticipate an attack from a second or more assailants. In delivering the Side Kick to your first assailant direct that kick to his knee or even shin area if you are not very flexible. Notice that after that kick, while you turn to face your second assailant, you must keep some pull on the left arm of your first assailant. This will aid you to keep your balance as you deal with your second assailant. However, if your kick drops your first assailant to the ground, do not try to hold him. Let him fall. In the upper left picture on page 58, stepping to meet the rear assailant can be modified by placing your right foot immediately next to your left foot, if he is closer than shown. *Do not* step your right leg behind your left leg in this case.

Situation: Two assailants have rammed you up against a wall by seizing your lapels. They threaten you with their free hands. There is no room to move backward.

Response: The assailant on your left attempts to strike you in the face with his left hand. Quickly dodge your head slightly away from the blow and with your left arm, drive a quick Sweeping Block, hand held in Knife-hand fashion, into the attacking left arm of the assailant at a point near his wrist. Form your right hand into a tight fist and keep it ready. (See pictures above.)

62

The assailant on your right attempts to slam a right into your mid-section. Quickly step your right foot slightly forward as shown in the diagram and, with your right arm, drive a hard Pressing Block against his attacking right arm. Maintain blocking contact with your left arm. (See pictures above.)

The assailant on your left breaks away and squares off for a new attack. Continue the Pressing Block action against the other assailant, but watch the assailant on your left. As he swings a right at you, deliver a hard Rising Block with your left arm against his striking right forearm. Pivot to face him as you continue to keep Pressing Block contact with your right arm against the assailant on your right. (Follow picture sequence, this page.)

Snap your left hand (which grasps the assailants right arm near his elbow) downward, bringing his right arm down and unbalancing him. Immediately break your Pressing Block contact and quickly step and pivot as shown in the diagram, delivering a hard Forward Elbow Strike to the midsection of the assailant on your left. (See pictures this page.)

Without hesitation, deliver a Side Kick to the assailant in the rear by weighting your right leg, knee slightly bent, and thrusting hard into his knee or shin area of either leg (left shown) with your left Side Foot. Keep your left hand grasp on the front assailants' right arm and ready your right tight fist for additional attack if necessary. These two actions can be seen on page 66.

65

Key Points: It is important to tie up one assailant (Pressing Block) and *maintain* the block until you can deal with the other assailant. Seek to blend all the movements into a smooth technique with a minimum of movement. Be sure to drop your hips as you make blocking contact.

Situation: You are walking along and are suddenly seized in a lapel grasp by an assailant from your right side. His partner is closing in on you from your left and is preparing to kick you.

67

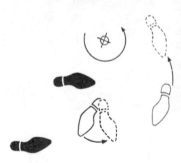

Response: As the assailant grasps your right lapel from your right side, move quickly into a right Forward Stance with a Front-facing Posture. Immediately step your left foot back circularly to your rear as you pivot your right foot a bit to your left. (See the diagram.) Simultaneous with this action, push your right shoulder hard against the outside of the assailant's grasping left arm by twisting your hips to your left. This will make any right hand blow of his ineffective. Drop your hips a bit as you do this. (See pictures this page.)

Quickly twist your body back to your right as you deliver a hard
Bottom Fist or Knife-hand to that assailant's rib area or solar plexus.
Keep your body low as you strike to avoid any possible striking from
the assailant. (See picture above.)

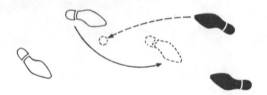

Turn a bit to your left to meet the second assailants' kicking attack. Step forward with your left foot and keep your body in a Half-front-facing Posture. (See diagram.) Begin to swing a hard Downward Block against the second assailant's kicking right leg, using your left arm, fist held tightly. (See pictures above.)

Deliver a hard Downward Block to the right kicking leg of the second assailant, making contact at any point between his ankle and his knee. (See picture above.) Withdraw your right arm alongside of your right hip, hand held in a tight fist, knuckles downward.

Your Downward Block will also deflect the assailant's kick and enable you to deliver a hard right Fore Fist to his midsection with your right hand as you twist your hips to your left as you strike. This action can be seen on page 72. After striking, keep alert for a continuation of their attack.

Key Points: Using your right shoulder to block the first assailant's grasping arm, and any blow he might try with his right hand, requires you to twist, step, and block in unison. In the final striking to the second assailant's midsection, it may be necessary for you to step forward into him in order to strike your target.

Situation: You have been grabbed from the rear by one assailant who is pulling you backward by the collar of your coat. His partner is closing in on you from the front and is preparing to strike you.

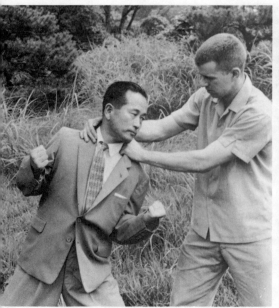 

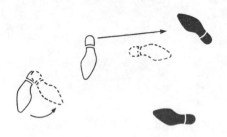

Response: As the rear assailant grabs your collar and pulls you backward, do not struggle to shake his grasp, but blend with his pull and twist your body to the left by pivoting a bit on your right foot and stepping your left foot in between the rear assailant's feet. (See diagram.) As you twist and step, form both your hands into a tight fist and simultaneously deliver your left fist to the rear assailant's groin or solar plexus, and your right fist directly to his facial area. (See pictures above.) This complete action can be seen at the top of page 75.

74

After striking simultaneously with both fists, shift your full weight onto your left leg, knee bent. Draw your right leg, knee bent, upward near your body, thigh parallel to the ground. (See pictures on this page.) Turn your face to watch the second assailant closing in on you and deliver a hard Foot Edge kick to his groin or knee with your right leg. The completed action can be seen on page 76. Keep alert for a continuation of their attack.

Key Points: If at the rear assailant's grasp you try to break loose from him, you may invite trouble. Seek to blend your body twist and stepping so that you are able to strike him simultaneously with both fists. Be sure to bring your right leg up close to your body, thigh parallel to the ground, before you deliver your Foot Edge kick.

Situation: Two assailants have seized you, each one holding one of your arms, and have backed you up against a wall so there is little chance of escaping. Their partner is closing in on you from the front and is preparing to kick you.

Response: As the two side assailants hold you, give them some struggle so as to keep them busy holding you. At the approach of the front assailant, keep alert and watch carefully for his kick. As he lashes out with his right foot, reach out with your right foot and hook your instep behind the back of his leg from the inside just above his heel. (See top left picture.) Scoop up his kicking leg with your right foot and twist your hips to your left as you do this. The scooping action will bring him off balance. (See top right picture.) Study picture sequence above.

78

Immediately deliver a hard front snap kick using the tip of your shoe or the ball of your foot to the frontal assailant's groin. This action can be seen in the picture above.

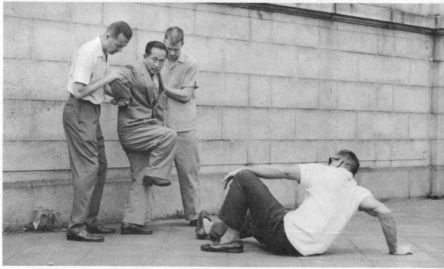

As your frontal assailant is kicked, quickly bring your right foot under you, thigh parallel to the ground, and without hesitation stamp hard against the right assailant's instep, using your Foot Edge with the right foot to deliver this blow. (Follow the pictures on this page and the top picture on page 81.)

Follow this kick quickly with a hard Back Fist, using your right hand to the right assailant's facial area as he loosens his grip on you after your kick. (See picture above.) Quickly twist your body to the left and deliver a hard Front Knee Kick to the assailant on the left, aiming for his groin region. This action can be seen on page 82. Keep alert for a continuation of any of their attacks.

Key Points: You must absolutely time your right foot scooping with the kick of the frontal assailant's right foot. The scooping action is a big circular action which climbs from a low position to a high position as you scoop his leg upward and in toward yourself, but away to your left and out of line with your vital areas. If you miss this scoop, your doubled right leg will serve as protection for you against his kick.

Chapter Two
ATTACKS AGAINST
SITTING POSITIONS

SIMILAR TO attack methods against standing positions, unarmed assailants working in pairs or small groups commonly make victims of those who are seated. Their tactics include seizing, holding the arms or portions of the garments, hugging, choking, and encirclement, while the second or other members of the group endeavor to threaten you with further violence that may include searching, punching or striking, or combinations of these methods. All can be used with effective results against an untrained individual.

Being attacked by multiple unarmed assailants as you sit, greatly decreases your chances for a successful defense, and an improper response by you may result in serious injury.

Persons highly trained in *karate* techniques are able to face such situations with a high degree of confidence, yet the difference between the highly trained *karate* expert and Mr. Average Citizen is great. The situations and the appropriate responses shown in this chapter have been selected especially for the man on the street and cover the necessary principles to successfully meet common eventualities connected with unarmed multiple assailant attacks against seated positions.

Practice all responses with partners. During your initial practices begin slowly and gradually increase the speed of the "attack" and your response. Seek to build automatic responses. If you will practice a few minutes a day, several days a week, this development will be greatly aided.

Perform all your actions in normal daily dress. Do not make the mistake of practicing only on a smooth, flat surface such as a gym floor, but try to make these responses on grass, gravel, and paved and unpaved surfaces. This will bring you closer to reality . . . the situation as it could really happen.

The responses of this chapter are given in terms of one side, either on the right or left, but in most instances the other side may be learned by simply reversing the instructions.

Finally, some advice on the execution of the responses. The ideal situation of course is not to be caught seated! If at all possible, stand up prior to any threat of attack. When you do so, do not let your chair, bench, or stool remain behind you, but position yourself to one side of it or behind it. Perhaps, if it is a free object, it can become a weapon or obstacle in your favor. However, if you are caught seated and it is too late to rise, deal with the biggest threat first . . . and seek a chance to rise as your situation improves. Regardless of your plan of action, *never* assume that your first response will satisfy the situation. Rather assume a constant alertness which will enable you to continue your attack should it become necessary. The price of a lack of alertness may be your life! Make use of your study to determine other target areas than those recommended by the responses in this chapter.

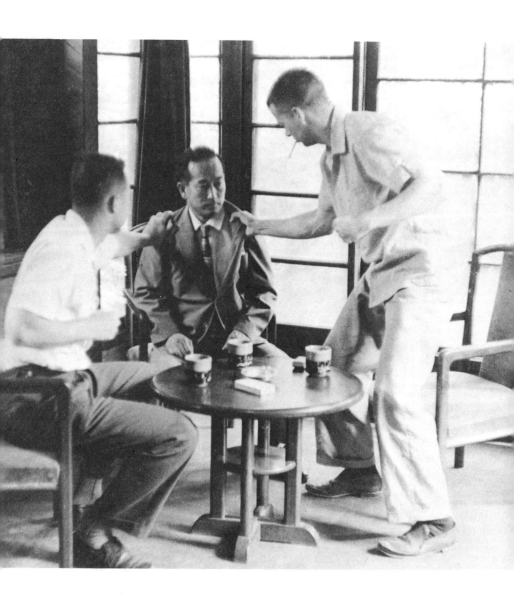

Situation: You are seated in a chair. Suddenly two seated assailants, one on each side of you, grab you by the lapels and begin to strike you.

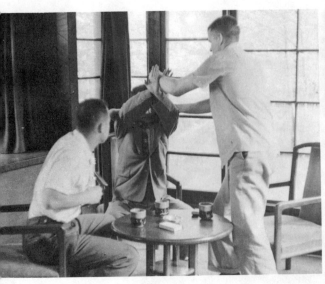

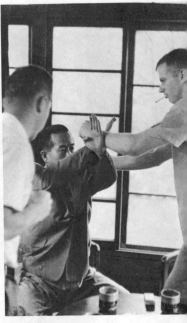

Response: The assailant on your left is on his feet and poses the greatest threat. As he strikes with a left, drive a hard **X**-Block under his striking arm, making contact at any point near his wrist, with either of your arms crossed foremost (left shown ahead of right). (See left picture above.) As you block the assailant on your left, the assailant on your right rises and begins to strike with his right. Watch him carefully. (See right picture above.) Immediately after your blocking action against the first assailant, catch his striking left arm in your right hand and pull his arm downward and forward to your right rear with a hard snap as you fold your left arm across your body, hand held in a tight fist, knuckles outward. As you snap his left arm downward, deliver a hard Bottom Fist to his left rib area with your left fist. This action can be seen in the right picture.

Release the first assailant and turn in your chair to meet the second assailant who is throwing a right at you. Block his blow upward with a right Rising Block, making contact anywhere along the underside of his striking arm. As you block, twist your body a bit to the left and withdraw your left arm alongside of your body, tight fist held at your left hip, knuckles down. This action can be seen in the picture above. Keeping your block in place, drive a hard Forward Strike, using your left arm, direct to the assailant's right rib or kidney area, coming up a bit out of your chair and twisting to your right as you do this. (See picture to the right.) The final action can be seen on page 88.

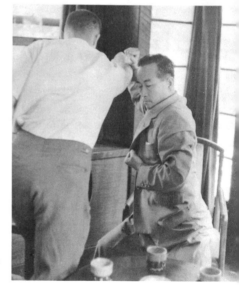

Key Points: Do not try to get up to meet either of the assailants. Stay low in your chair, feet braced under you as best you can. Your **X**-Block must be quickly turned into a grasp with your right hand as you snap the first assailant off balance. Twist your body a bit to your right, as you do this. This twist will also prepare you to meet the second assailant who is striking at you.

88

Situation: You are seated on a chair. Two assailants, one on each side of you, threaten you with striking. There is a low table in front of you.

Response: The assailant on your left comes to his feet first and begins to swing a left at you. If his blow is aimed at your face, drive a hard Rising Block against it, using your left arm at any point along his striking arm above his wrist. (See above left picture.) If the blow is aimed at your body, use the Sweeping Block with the same hand. Immediately catch his striking left arm with your left hand and pull him hard forward and downward (to your left rear) with a quick snap as you come out of your chair. Shift your full weight onto your bent left leg. Use your left hand pulling action on the assailant's left arm to bring you up out of your chair and, by pivoting a bit to your left on your left foot, swing your right leg around in "roundhouse" fashion, across the top of the low table, and deliver the tip of your shoe or the ball of your foot hard into the assailant's left rib or kidney region. This action can be seen in the right picture above.

90

Quickly withdraw your kicking right leg
and double up that leg, your weight full on
your bent left leg and slightly leaning away
from the assailant on your right. Keep your
left hand in contact with the first assailant's
left arm if possible. Apply a Sweeping Block,
using your right hand, to the second assailant's striking right arm at any point along
his arm near the wrist. (See picture to the
left.)

Quickly thrust your bent right leg into
the groin region of your second assailant,
using the heel of your Foot Edge into the
target. (See picture to the right.) The final
action can be seen on page 92. Keep alert
for continuation of their attack after kicking.

Key Points: Use your first blocking action against the assailant's striking arm to misdirect the striking, and the immediate catch of that arm to serve as a point to bring yourself out of the chair to deliver your first kick. Sometimes that first kick will turn you a bit and make the second kick with that leg difficult. If this happens, place your right foot on the floor and shift your weight to it, turning your back to the second assailant and then driving a hard heel kick into his groin.

92

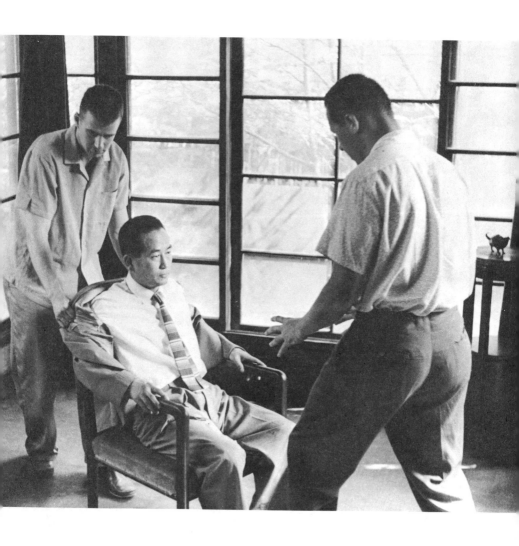

Situation: While seated in a chair, one assailant has grabbed and pulled your coat over the back of the chair, thereby pinning you in the chair. His partner is closing in on you from the front and is menacing you with search, kicking, choking, or striking.

93

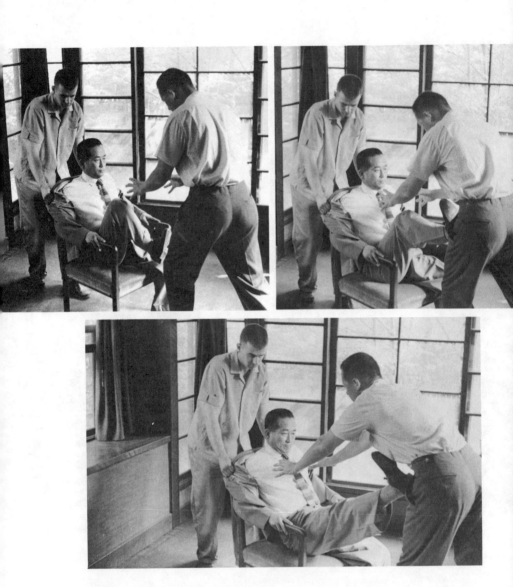

Response: The frontal assailant is the one to deal with first. Time his approach very carefully and, as he closes in on you, draw your right leg up close to your body by bending your knee. Make this a quick action. When the assailant is near enough, thrust your foot, sole first, directly into the assailant's groin region. (See pictures this page.)

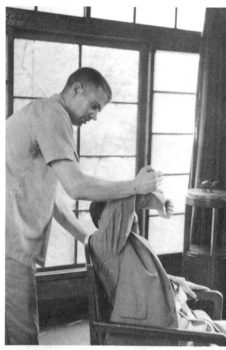

The rear assailant, now being left alone to attack you, releases his right hand grip and prepares to strike you with his open hand or fist in a chopping manner. (See picture above.) Drive your right arm, bent at the elbow, upward and backward to deflect his strike, making contact at any point along the underside of his arm near the wrist. (See upper picture to the right.) Immediately disengage the blocking action and deliver a hard Back Fist to the rear assailant's face by whipping your arm in a short arc upward. As the rear assailant is struck, he may release his other hand and and you are free to stand up quickly and keep alert for any continuation of their attack. This action can be seen on page 96.

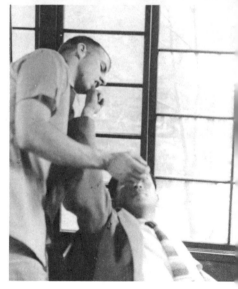

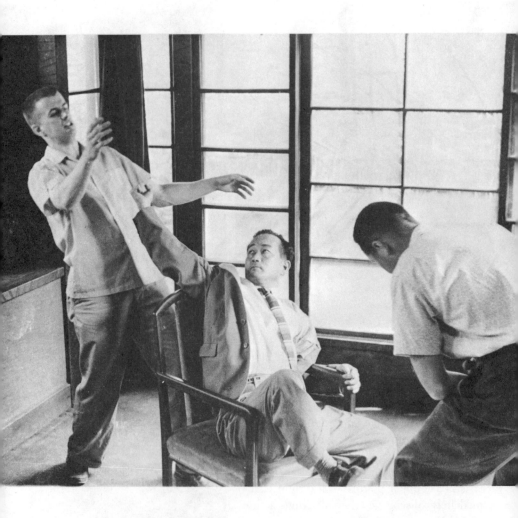

Key Points: Do not struggle to tear away from the assailant holding you in the chair. Concentrate on the frontal assailant closing in on you. Do not advertise your kicking action by making a slow doubling action, but rather time his approach well and double your right leg and kick with rapidity. Thrust with your heel as much as possible. The rear assailant is helpless and must release at least one hand to attack you. When he does, turn in your chair as much as you can to meet his striking attack and to deliver your Back Fist.

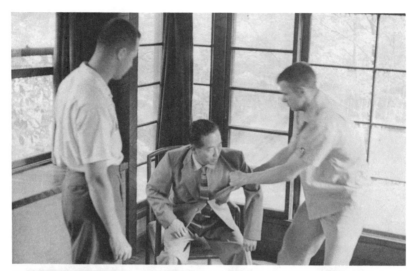

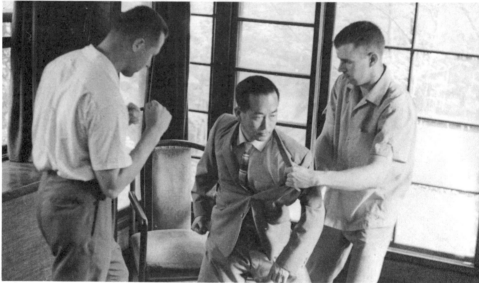

Situation: You are being pulled out of your chair by an assailant on your left who has seized you by your lapels and left arm. His partner is closing in on you from the other side and is preparing to strike you with his fists.

Response: As the assailant on your left pulls you up, blend your rising with his pull and come up faster than he expects. Swing your straightened right arm, hand held open, fingers together, in a big arc coming up from down low and across the assailant's eyes so that your finger tips just graze him. Twist your hips to your left as you do this and allow the arc of your right arm to pass beyond his face to his right side. The assailant will react by leaning backward and moving his face and head out of line with your raking action. (See picture sequence above.)

98

As your raking right hand passes his facial area, bend your right arm slightly and make a tight fist with your right hand. Deliver a hard Forward Elbow Strike into the assailant's solar plexus with your right arm as you withdraw your left arm alongside of your body, left hand coming to rest near your left hip, hand in a tight fist, knuckles down. (See pictures this page.)

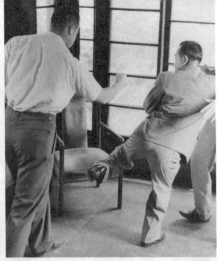

Quickly turn to your left to meet the other assailant who is closing in on you, watching him over your left shoulder. Shift your full weight onto your right leg, knee slightly bent, and bring your left leg up under you, knee bent. (Follow pictures this page.) Deliver a hard Foot Edge with your left foot to the rear assailant's groin, knee, or shin by thrusting your left leg directly into him. This action can be seen at the top of page 101.

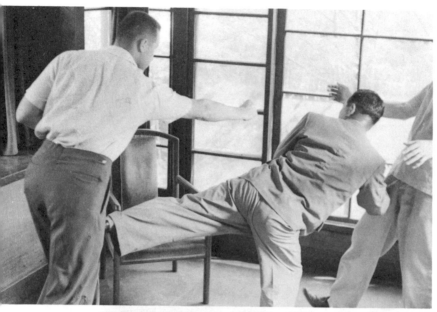

Immediately after kicking him, place your left foot on the ground, twist your body fully around to your left, press his right arm down from above with your left hand, and bring your right hand, held in a Knife-hand, near your right ear. (See picture above.) Deliver a hard Knife-hand to the side of the assailant's neck with your right hand as you twist fully into him with the force of the blow. This action can be seen on page 102. Keep alert after striking him.

Key Points: Your right arm raking action must be done with accuracy and not too fast. He must *see* the motion. If he fails to see it, due to speed, he may not react. Get your finger tips as close as possible to his eyes as they brush by his face. Time your striking actions with the twist of your body.

Chapter Three
ATTACKS AGAINST
LYING POSITIONS

OCCASIONALLY unarmed multiple assailants will attack a victim who is on the ground in a lying or semi-sitting position. These attacks take the form of encirclement, kicking or kneeing, seizing, holding the arms or portions of the garments, or choking while the second or other members of the small group endeavor to threaten the victim with further violence that includes searching, punching or striking, kneeing or kicking, or combinations of these tactics.

Regardless of how you happen to be on the ground—as the result of your assailant's attacks or by your own loss of balance as you fight to defend yourself—going down on the ground while engaged with multiple assailants *should not be a voluntary measure.* Once you are on the ground, your mobility is greatly reduced and you may suffer serious injury or even loss of life by determined assailants.

Persons highly trained in *karate* techniques can successfully cope with such situations, yet the difference between such a highly trained individual and the average man is tremendous. The situations and appropriate responses shown in this chapter are specially designed for the ordinary man and cover the necessary principles to efficiently meet common eventualities caused by unarmed multiple assailant attacks against a victim who is on the ground.

You must practice these responses with partners. Begin slowly by going slow motion through the situations and responses. Work the speed up to where you have an automatic reaction to each "attack" situation. A few minutes each day, several days per week, will help you to build confidence.

Practice only in normal daily dress. Do not give yourself the convenience of a smooth, flat surface such as a gym floor, but try to put realism in the training by getting out on grass, gravel, and paved and unpaved surfaces. In this way you will become familiar with the situation as it could really happen.

Responses in this chapter are given in terms of one side, operating either on the right or left, but in many instances the other side may be learned by simply reversing the instructions.

Some final advice may be helpful to you. If at all possible, stand up. Do not get caught on the ground by assailants, but if it is too late to rise, perform your responses always with the idea of looking for the chance to get up on your feet. Try not to let any of the assailants hold you down in any fashion as you will become a "punching bag" for the others. Keep moving, even if it is rather wild flailing and kicking, but remember that exertion while on the ground is more demanding than that used on your feet. Do not take a defensive position on "all fours," for you cannot see where your assailants are and what they are doing. Regardless of your plan of action, *do not* assume that your first response will satisfy the situation. Rather assume a constant alertness which will enable you to attack again and again should it become necessary. The price of a lack of alertness may be your life! Make use of your knowledge to find targets other than those sugested by the responses in this chapter.

Situation: You are menaced by two assailants, one on each side. The assailant on your right has grasped your lapel and is preparing to strike you as his partner stands by, waiting his opportunity to trip you to the ground.

Response: The assailant who has grabbed you from your right side strikes at you with a straight right hand. At his striking motion, drop your hips by bending your knees and step directly into him with your right foot coming to rest between his feet, and drive a hard Rising Block against his striking arm, making contact at any point above his elbow. With this blocking action, withdraw your left arm alongside of your body, hand held in a tight fist, knuckles down, at your left hip. (See diagram and top left picture.)

Upon completion of your blocking action, twist your body to the right and deliver a hard Forward Elbow Strike to the assailant's solar plexus, rib area or kidney region using your left arm. (See pictures to the right and below.)

As you strike the assailant with your elbow, the other assailant kicks your left foot out from under you and you fall to the ground. (See above pictures.) As you land, the assailant who has tripped you closes in and is striking at you with his left hand. As you hit the ground, immediately roll onto your left side and double your left foot under you. Block the assailant's left hand attack with a Sweeping Block, applied by your right hand at any point along the inside of his attacking left arm near his wrist, Simultaneously bring your right leg up close to your body, bending the knee, and then quickly thrust your right sole hard into the assailant's groin, midsection, or rib area. (See lower right picture above.) The final action can be seen on page 108.

Key Points: When you turn to block your first assailant, drive forward off your left leg and come up under the assailant's strike. Do not separate the arm blocking action and the force of your body coming forward. Be sure to draw your left leg under you as you hit the ground. Get up quickly when the chance comes.

108

Situation: You have been seized by two assailants, one on each side of you, and they are pushing you up against a wall. They try to knock you down at the base of the wall and plan to kick you.

Response: If you cannot break free from their initial pushing attack, and are forced against the wall and knocked down, keep your back to the wall and your legs drawn up close to you. (See top left.) As the assailant on your right begins to kick at you, swing a hard right Downward Block at his kicking leg, hand held in a tight fist, and make contact behind his leg near his ankle. This action will misdirect his kick and make him step forward with his right kicking leg. (Follow pictures this page.)

As the assailant on your left kicks at you, anticipate the kick by turning slightly to your left and reaching your left arm forward to the inside of his kicking left leg. (See top picture.) Make a scooping action with this hand and catch his kicking left foot behind the heel as you pull his leg forward into yourself. Simultaneously drive your right hand hard against his kicking knee and lift his kicking leg as you work your hands in Scooping Block fashion to upset his balance. (See three pictures above.)

Twist his kicking leg to your left and turn him around by leverage and pressure against his ankle and knee. (See pictures.)

As he turns and is pushed a bit forward by you, quickly drop into the place along the base of the wall, retaining your grips on his left leg for support. You drop onto your left side and double your right leg up close to your body as you deliver a hard Foot Edge using your right foot to the first assailant's knee or shin. (See picture below.) The final action can be seen on page 114.)

Key Points: When you block with a Downward Block against the first assailant, you can strike him with a Bottom Fist on the back of his leg at the calf, or just above his heel. You must get him to step forward and be off balance with this blocking action. Your left hand scooping action against the second assailant's kick must not wait for his kick. You must reach out and behind his kicking foot quickly. When you fall onto your left side, be sure to use your left elbow and arm to support yourself when you deliver a strong kicking action against the first assailant. You may do this and still retain your grip on the second assailant's left leg, pinning it onto the ground. Get up quickly when the chance comes.

Situation: You have been knocked to the ground and one assailant is kneeling alongside of you and is choking you with both hands. His partner is standing at your left side and is trying to kick you or stomp you.

115

Response: The assailant who is choking you must be dealt with first. Draw your left leg up and swing your knee hard into his exposed right rib area. Twist a bit to your right as you do this, but do not try to move your neck or break his choking actions. Keep his hands occupied. Immediately after kneeing him, quickly thrust your right hand, hand held as a Hand Spear, into his facial area, aiming for his eyes. This thrust must be between his choking arms and should be as hard as possible. (Follow picture sequence on the next page.)

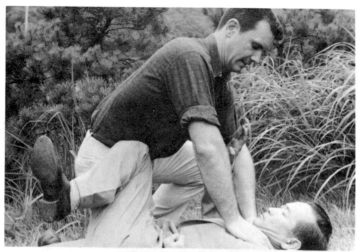

Your Hand Spear attack, even if it does not strike the target, will loosen his choking attack and make a second chance for you to sit up a bit as you drive repeated Hand Spears into his face. (See picture above.)

As you attack his face, hold your left hand, held in a tight fist, ready. (See picture above.)

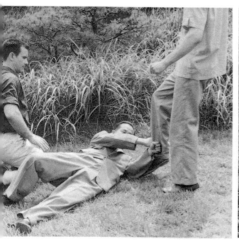 

Turn to meet the second assailant's kicking attack by rolling slightly onto your left side. Deliver your left fist, held either as a Back Fist or a Bottom Fist, hard against his kicking right shin as you roll up onto your left shoulder. Also punch your right Fore Fist above your left arm and straight into his shin. This double punching action acts as a block against his kick. (See pictures.) Quickly grasp his trouser leg with your right hand and pull him to your right across your body as you double your left leg under you and bend your right leg to kick. Deliver a hard snap kick, using the point of your right shoe, to his groin region. (See picture at right.) This final action can be seen on page 120. Get up to your feet quickly and be prepared for a continuation of their attack.

Key Points: Do not try to move away from the choking action of the assailant. Your kneeing action serves to loosen him up for your Hand Spear, but if he kneels too far from you, a snap kick with either your left or right foot may do the job. Knee or kick first, then spear. You may have time to sit up a bit to meet the second assailant, but don't count on it. Pull hard on the assailant's trousers to unbalance him.